How to Yo-Yo

Tricks & Tips to Make Everyone a Champion

Larry Sayco

ILLUSTRATED BY **Evan Yarbrough**

Mud Puddle inc.

NEW YORK

How To Yo-Yo:
Tricks & Tips to Make Everyone a Champion

Written by Larry Sayco
Illustrated by Evan Yarbrough

Copyright © 1998 by Larry Sayco
Illustrations copyright © 2007 by Mud Puddle, Inc.

Originally published in 1998 as
The Ultimate Yo-Yo Book

Published by
Mud Puddle, Inc.
36 W. 25th Street
New York, NY 10010
info@mudpuddleinc.com

ISBN: 978-1-60311-113-3

Printed in China, May 2018

9 10 8

CONTENTS

TRICKS, TIPS AND TROUBLESHOOTING

The Basics

The Tricks

Ten Tips for Getting Started

1 Weight matters! Make sure your yo-yo isn't too light. A good yo-yo needs to weigh at least an ounce.

2 For best results, go for the plain! Use a simple, undecorated yo-yo. Avoid a yo-yo that lights up, whistles, hums, recites a poem or does anything fancy.

3 Resist temptation: don't take your yo-yo apart. For the mechanically inclined, there are special yo-yos meant to be taken apart and if you need to know what makes your yo-yo tick, buy one of these.

4 Customize your yo-yo. Unwind the string and stand the yo-yo on the floor in front of you. Have a grown-up cut the string even with your chest. The string will appear to be a little too long, but when you tie a finger loop, it should be just right—touching the bottom of your belly-button.

5 Always begin your yo-yo adventuring by tying a small loop at the end of the string. By pulling part of the string through the loop each time you yo-yo, you've created an easy slipknot.

6 The slipknot loop goes on your *middle finger*. Beginners should always put the loop right next to their hand. More advanced players should keep the loop between the first and second knuckle.

7 You want a slipknot that fits tightly over your finger while you are playing but opens up easily when you want to take it off. If your finger begins to hurt or the string stops your blood flow, take a break for a while. If you want, you can wrap a band-aid around your finger and put the loop over the band-aid.

BEGINNER

ADVANCED

8 Become familiar with a trick before you attempt it. Read the directions and make certain you understand them. If you don't, ask for help.

9 Learn to walk before you run! Master the easy tricks before moving on to the harder ones. You master a trick by learning each step before moving on to the next step.

10 **Most important:** always BE CAREFUL when using a yo-yo, even if you're alone. If you're doing the tricks in front of other people, make certain you tell them to stand back!

Knot Know-How

○ If you have trouble with knots, don't be discouraged. This is a problem shared by all yo-yo players whether beginner or pro. These tips will help you.

○ Knots won't undo themselves. There's no need to swing or dangle the yo-yo hoping for a miracle.

○ Remember, pulling on the ends of the string or on the yo-yo itself can only make matters worse.

○ Absolutely, *NEVER* use a knife to try to undo a knot. It won't help and it's DANGEROUS!!!

○ One good way to open a knot tangled in the yo-yo is to open up one end of a paperclip and use it to pick open the knot. If you're having trouble with this, ask an adult help you.

○ If the string is knotted, look at it closely to see how it's knotted. Then try to pick the knot open. Remember—knots require patience!

ONE LAST TIP:

When you buy a yo-yo, pick up some extra string. If your string breaks, wears out, or is so badly knotted that you have to cut it, you'll be ready. Follow the manufacturer's directions for replacing the string.

Kinks

If the yo-yo string twists too tight, it will form tiny beads. This is known as pig-tailing and the beads are known as kinks. This is easy to fix. Just let the yo-yo drop to the end of the string and untwist itself. If you untwist too much it will slip and be hard to wind, so you have to toss it back down and twist to the right or clockwise 5 turns at a time until it winds easily.

String Cleaning

After eating, always wash your hands before you play with your yo-yo again, even if you've only had a snack, like chips or cookies. Food grease on the string can sometimes make the yo-yo slip. If the string does get dirty, remove it. Ask a grown-up to pin it to one of your white shirts, and toss it in the laundry machine. When the string dries, it will look and feel like new!

Winding the Yo-Yo

Wrap each turn by hand. If you are left-handed, wrap the string toward you. If you're right-handed, wrap it away from you. If the string doesn't catch, try this: pinch the string about 2 inches above the yo-yo. Wind with the string slack until it starts to catch.

Single or Double Axle Loops

Inside the groove of a yo-yo, the string is looped around the axle. The string can be either single looped or double looped around the axle. Beginners generally find it easier to learn on a yo-yo that is double looped. However, since you can't do any of the sleeper tricks with the yo-yo double looped, switch over to a single loop as soon as your skills permit.

Making the switch from double looped to single is simple. Just hold the string tightly and untwist the yo-yo to the left (counter clockwise) until you see two separate strings. Open the space between the strings and pass the yo-yo through it. Now your yo-yo is single looped. If the yo-yo doesn't return when you pull it up, simply tighten the string by twisting the yo-yo to the right (clockwise).

Down and Up

○ Hold the yo-yo in your hand like a ball. Your palm should be down and about even with your bellybutton, but not touching your body.

○ Open your hand and let the yo-yo drop toward the floor. As soon as you open your hand, say "Yo-Yo".

○ After the second "Yo," smoothly lift your yo-yo hand up about 3 or 4 inches. You'll feel a snap when the yo-yo reaches the bottom of the string and because of your tug, the yo-yo will climb up the opposite side of the string.

○ When the yo-yo reaches the top of the string, close your hand quickly to catch it.

Down and Up Trouble Tips

Problem   Yo-yo wobbles sideways.
Cause   Yo-yo isn't heavy enough
What to Do   Until you get a heavier one, tape a penny on the center of each side of the yo-yo.

Problem   Yo-yo keeps going sideways and the weight of the yo-yo is not the problem.
Cause   You're pushing the yo-yo down when you open your hand.
What to Do   Open your hand gently but quickly to let the yo-yo fall to Mother Earth.

Problem   Yo-yo goes down okay, but doesn't come up all the way, or doesn't come up at all.
Cause   Your tug timing is slightly off.
What to Do   Instead of saying Yo-Yo, try counting. Open on "One," pull up on "Two," catch on "three."

Problem   Yo-yo returns to your hand, but with a hand full of spaghetti (unwound string).
Cause   You're grabbing the yo-yo too soon.
What to Do   Wait until the yo-yo touches your hand before you snap it shut.

11

The Bouncing Yo-Yo

○ This trick is based on the basic Down and Up. It's a little harder, but fun to practice!

○ Open your hand and let the yo-yo fall.

○ Tug up on the string. However, when the yo-yo returns to your hand, don't try to catch it.

○ Keep your hand flat and give the yo-yo a gentle pat to make it go back down.

○ Repeat until you feel like catching it.

HOW MANY TIMES CAN YOU DO IT?

Once you get the timing down on this trick, it's almost like bouncing a ball. You can do it forever—or at least until the string breaks or your finger falls off!

NOW: BE A SHOW-OFF!

○ Try the Bouncing Yo-Yo standing on one foot.

○ Try the Bouncing Yo-Yo with your eyes closed. No peeking!

○ Try the Bouncing Yo-Yo with your eyes closed and standing on one foot. If you can do this, you're really good. Most people can't do this even without the yo-yo!

The Forward Pass

Practice this trick without the yo-yo a couple of times to get the feel of it.

○ Pretend you are about to throw a bowling ball. If you're right-handed, stand with your right foot slightly out in front. If you're left-handed, stand with your left foot slightly out in front.

○ Put your yo-yo hand, palm up, as far back as you can. Keep your wrist curled.

○ Swing your arm forward, uncurling your wrist. Let go of the yo-yo when your hand is even with your forward toe. This will send the yo-yo out in front of you at an angle.

○ Once the yo-yo is completely out of your hand, turn your hand so your palm faces the ceiling.

○ The yo-yo will spin to the end of the string, reverse itself, and return to your hand, where you can catch it.

Forward Pass Trouble Tips

Problem   Yo-yo twists when it leaves your hand.
Cause   You're twisting your hand too soon.
What to Do   Make sure the yo-yo is completely out of your hand before the twist. Try counting again. Throw on "One," and twist on "Two."

Problem   You can't catch the yo-yo on its return.
Cause   You're throwing either too hard or too soft.
What to Do   A fast throw can be tough to catch. A soft throw won't make it all the way back. Adjust the speed of your throw.

Problem   Yo-yo goes out straight, but returns too high to catch.
Cause   You're releasing the yo-yo too late.
What to Do   Remember to let go of the yo-yo when your hand passes your forward toe.

See how many Forward Passes in a row you can throw!

Loop the Loop

○ A single Loop the Loop is sometimes tough for beginners to learn, but it is the basis for all the other looping tricks.

○ Stand and throw the yo-yo the same way you did for the Forward Pass.

○ When the yo-yo comes back, don't catch it. Instead, direct the yo-yo between your arm and your body, making a circle with your wrist. This is almost like waving someone to come back, except you follow all the way around with a swift snap.

○ The yo-yo will make a loop or large circle and return to your hand where you can either catch it or guide it back out with another snap of your wrist.

Loop the Loop Tips

○ If you are having trouble, re-read the directions carefully.

○ Remove the yo-yo from your finger and practice the wrist motion until you get the hang of it.

○ DON'T be scared of the yo-yo.

○ Try doing the Forward Pass several times in a row. When you see a really excellent one coming back at you, GO FOR IT!

○ DON'T give up. Keep trying until you get the hang of it. You're going to feel proud for doing this difficult trick by yourself!

Once you can do a perfect loop every time, try for two in a row. Then three or four! See how many you can do without stopping!

The Sleeper

○ Curl your hand, bend your elbow and make a muscle like Popeye, but with your arm in front of you.

○ Give your hand, fingers, wrist and arm a downward whipping motion—as if you're shaking water off your hand— throwing the yo-yo out and down.

○ As you throw the yo-yo, lift your hand 3 or 4 inches, and then turn it so the palm faces the ground. If you do this right, the yo-yo will spin at the bottom of the string.

○ Give the string a quick upward tug to make the yo-yo return.

○ Catch it.

Sleeper Trouble Tips

Problem   Yo-yo sleeps but won't come back up.
Cause   String is too loose.
What to Do   Tighten by unwinding the yo-yo, then twisting it to the right (clockwise) about 20 times. Wind and try again.

Problem   Yo-yo won't spin. It returns as soon as you throw it.
Cause   String is too tight.
What to Do   Loosen string by unwinding the yo-yo and letting it untwist to the left (counterclockwise).
OR Cause   You're throwing the yo-yo wrong.
What to Do   Throw the yo-yo out and just leave it there. Don't tug or jerk the string at all.

Problem   Yo-yo slants to one side.
Cause   You're turning your hand too soon.
What to Do   Make sure the yo-yo is completely out of your hand before you turn it.
OR Cause   Yo-yo isn't spinning fast enough.
What to Do   Try throwing it harder with more of a snap.
OR Cause   You're slanting the throw.
What to Do   Practice in a room with straight lines on the floor. Stand with your feet parallel to the lines. Then throw the yo-yo so that it also spins parallel to those lines.

zzzz...

"Lots of tricks are based on Sleepers. Here are some fun ones to try. They're especially good to show off in front of your friends or family."

Hint: When doing tricks in front of people, always tell them the name of the trick before you do it! It will be easier for them to remember and they will enjoy it more.

Spank the Baby

○ Throw a good, fast, straight sleeper.

○ While it's spinning say, "Naughty baby."

○ Then use your free hand to slap or spank the back of your yo-yo hand. That should be enough of a jerk to make the yo-yo return.

○ Catch it.

When you do a sleeper trick, make sure the yo-yo is spinning straight and fast enough to finish the trick. If it isn't, catch it, or it might die in the middle!

Spank the Baby Twice

This looks better if you do Spank the Baby first.

○ Throw a good, fast, straight sleeper.

○ With your free hand, spank the baby twice, but not hard enough to bring the yo-yo back up. Say, "I spanked the baby twice, but he didn't wake up."

○ Make a fist with your free hand and poke it hard upward into the palm of your yo-yo hand. Say, "So I gave him a poke in the tummy!"

○ When the yo-yo comes back up, catch it.

The Karate Chop

○ Start just like Spank the Baby.

○ Instead of giving your hand a spank, give the knuckles of your yo-yo hand a karate chop, yelling, "Hi-YA!"

○ When the yo-yo comes up, catch it.

Don't overdo it. Remember, it's your own hand you're karate chopping!

The Bow and Arrow

○ Throw another good, fast sleeper.

○ While the yo-yo is sleeping, lift your yo-yo hand high so the middle part of the string is at eye level, but away from your body.

○ Squint like you're taking aim. Then with your free hand, pluck the middle of the string as if it were a guitar.

○ As soon as you pluck the string, the yo-yo should come up. Catch it, and say, "Bull's-eye!"

The Buzz Saw

○ Crumple up a piece of scrap paper and put it on the floor in front of you.

○ Throw a fast sleeper.

○ Lightly skim the spinning yo-yo over the top of the paper. You will hear it make a buzzing noise.

○ Before it spins out, give the string a tug and catch the yo-yo.

○ Don't be a litterbug. Throw away or recycle the paper when you're done!

The Cuckoo Clock

○ Throw a good sleeper.

○ Hold your yo-yo hand in one place. and make the yo-yo swing back and forth like the pendulum of a large clock. Say, "Tick-Tock, Tick-Tock."

○ Bring the yo-yo back up. When you catch it say, "Cuckoo!"

See how many times you can swing the yo-yo back and forth and still catch it.

Seven-Up

○ Throw a real hard sleeper.

○ When it starts to spin, count "1, 2, 3, 4, 5, 6, 7, and up!"

○ When you say "up!" tug the string and catch the yo-yo.

At first you may have to count fast, but as you get better, you'll be able to count even higher than 7!

Take A Hike

○ Throw a fast sleeper.

○ Walk a few steps forward, turn around, and come back to where started.

○ Bring the yo-yo up and catch it.

See how far you can go and come back, while still making a smooth catch at the end. Just be careful not to bump into anything!

Walk the Dog

○ Start with a very fast, straight sleeper.

○ Move your yo-yo hand directly above the yo-yo. This should stop its swinging.

○ When the string is straight up and down, gently lower the yo-yo to the floor, letting it barely skim over the ground.

○ The spin of the yo-yo will move it across the floor. Guide it with your yo-yo hand.

○ Tug the string to bring the yo-yo back up. Then catch it.

For fun, find a few friends and hold a Walk the Dog race. Who can go the farthest? It doesn't count if the yo-yo stops or you don't catch it with all the string wound up inside.

Walk the Dog Troubleshooting

Problem   Yo-yo touches the floor and comes up immediately.
Cause   String is too tight.
What to Do   Loosen the string (see page 19).
or Cause   Yo-yo is hitting the floor too hard or at an angle.
What to Do   The string must be **straight** up and down before you **gently** lower the yo-yo.

Take care of your yo-yo!

DON'T walk your yo-yo over the cement. Cement can chew up the edges.

DON'T walk it over the ground outside. Pebbles, sand, or dirt might get stuck in the groove. Blades of grass can get caught between the string and the axle.

DON'T walk your yo-yo through a puddle. Water is very bad for yo-yos.

The best place for your yo-yo is over a wood floor, or a short, not so shaggy carpet.

Fire Hydrant ZigZag

You'll need six empty soda cans for this trick.

○ Stand the soda cans in a line. They should be 6 inches apart.

○ Pretending each can is a fire hydrant, Walk the Dog, zigzagging through the space between each can.

○ See how many cans you can go by without knocking any over. (If the yo-yo moves or touches a can, that's okay, as long as the can stays standing.)

○ Bring the yo-yo up and catch it.

Hit or Miss

You'll need one clean, dry, empty soda can for this trick.

○ Stand the soda can up beside you.

○ Throw a good, hard sleeper and let the yo-yo swing toward the can.

○ Try to make the swinging yo-yo miss the can as it swings forward, but knock over the can on the return swing.

○ Bring the yo-yo back up and catch it.

Seems easy, right?
It's harder than you think.

Half Moon

○ Hold the yo-yo as you would for a sleeper except hold your arm to your side.

○ Make sure there is nothing near you on that side.

○ Curl your wrist as much as you can to start, then uncurl it as you throw a sleeper sideways.

○ When the yo-yo reaches the end of the string, swing it in a half-circle in front of you.

○ Give the string a tug when the yo-yo reaches the height of your other shoulder.

○ Hold your yo-yo hand palm up and catch the yo-yo.

Half Moon Trouble Tips

Problem   Yo-yo won't sleep.
Cause   String is too tight.
What to Do   Loosen string (see page 19).
OR Cause   You're throwing wrong.
What to Do   Throw the yo-yo both high and sideways.

Problem   You have trouble catching the yo-yo after the trick.
Cause   You're throwing the yo-yo too hard or too soft.
What to Do   Adjust the speed of the throw.
OR Cause   Your catching hand is in the wrong position.
What to Do   Stand with your yo yo hand about waist high,
palm facing the yo-yo, knuckles toward the ground.

Eating Spaghetti

○ Throw a fast, straight sleeper.

○ While the yo-yo is sleeping, bunch up the string with both hands to within 3 inches of the yo-yo.

○ Put all the bunched-up string in your yo-yo hand, leaving your other hand free.

○ Pretend you are sprinkling cheese and sauce on your handful of spaghetti, then hold it in front of your mouth.

○ Let go of all the string while making a slurping sound. If the yo-yo is spinning fast enough, the string will disappear into the yo-yo, and everyone will think you slurped up all the spaghetti in just one gulp.

○ Catch the yo-yo, then rub your belly. Delicious!

The Tumbling Tower

You'll need four empty soda cans for this trick.

○ Stack the cans, one on top of the other.

○ Throw a hard sleeper, then swing the yo-yo, trying to knock the top can off the tower.

○ With each swing, try to knock only one can off the tower at a time.

○ When you've knocked over the last can, tug on the string and catch the yo-yo.

Try this trick with a friend—take turns knocking a can off the tower. (Be careful not to hit each other!)

Yo-Yo Bowling

You'll need ten clean, empty cans to go bowling!

○ Set up the cans in a triangle, like the pins at a bowling alley.

○ Stand about 2 or 3 feet in front of the first can.

○ Throw a straight sleeper and gently remove the finger loop from your finger.

○ Lower the yo-yo to the ground as if you were Walking the Dog.

○ When it starts to "walk," let go of the string.

See how many cans you knock over!

The Creeper

○ Throw a fast sleeper and let it swing as in the Cuckoo Clock.

○ When the yo-yo swings out in front of you as far as it can go, squat down quickly and put your yo-yo hand, palm down, on the floor. The yo-yo should sleep on the floor in front of you.

○ Give the string a quick tug to make the yo-yo creep across the floor to your hand. Then catch it.

Here's a tip: Keep the yo-yo as close to the floor a possible when swinging it out. If the yo-yo is higher than a foot off the floor, don't try the trick. Just catch it and try again. Remember: a hard enough hit can seriously damage the yo-yo.

The Statue of Liberty

You'll need one empty soda can for this patriotic trick. Make sure the can is clean and very dry or you may end up with sticky soda running down your arm. Yuck!

○ Hold the can upside down in your free hand.

○ Throw a fast sleeper on the *side*, not out front. Make sure the flat side of the yo-yo is toward you.

○ Let the yo-yo swing once. As it comes up, try to land the yo-yo—still spinning—on top of the can.

○ While whistling, humming, or singing a few lines of your favorite patriotic song, raise the can with the yo-yo on it above your head. Stand in a Statue of Liberty pose.

○ To catch the yo-yo, push the can up toward the ceiling, then quickly pull the can out of the way.

○ Catch the yo-yo in your yo-yo hand.

The Statue of Liberty Trouble Tips

Problem   Yo-yo bounces off the can instead of landing there.

Cause   You're holding the can too stiffly.

What to Do   Relax! As the yo-yo drops down on the can, lower the can a little to absorb the shock.

Problem   Yo-yo spins a short time on the can, but then jerks back to your yo-yo hand.

Cause   Too much slack on the string.

What to Do   While the yo-yo is spinning on the can, keep the string sort of tight.

Problem   After you do the trick, you can't catch the yo-yo.

Cause   Yo-yo hand is in the wrong position.

What to Do   Catch the yo-yo overhand, not underhand. The tip of your yo-yo finger should point to the ceiling, not the ground.

Around the World

○ Start the trick as a Forward Pass but swing your arm a little higher in front of you, stopping when your hand is at about the height of your shoulder. (Don't turn your hand as you usually would for a Forward Pass.)

○ The yo-yo should move up and back, making a large circle outside your arm.

○ When the yo-yo completes the circle, turn your hand around and give the yo-yo a tug to wake it up.

○ Catch the yo-yo.

Warning!!! Be sure no one is standing behind or in front of you, and that there are no pets or glass objects within range!

Around the World Trouble Tips

Problem   When you throw the yo-yo out, it just comes right back.
Cause   String is too tight.
What to Do Loosen string (see page 19).
OR Cause   You're throwing wrong.
What to Do The trick only starts like a Forward Pass. Aim more for the ground as you swiftly uncurl your wrist toward the sky.

Don't try doing more than one Around the World at a time. If you try for more than one orbit on a single throw, the string may snap. Then it would be time to start saving for a new yo-yo!

The Bunny Hop

○ Throw a fast, hard sleeper but don't turn your hand as you normally would.

○ While the yo-yo sleeps, place the elbow of your yo-yo hand in front of the string.

○ With the string touching the back of your arm, bring your hand down and lift your elbow to the height of your shoulder.

○ Curl the wrist of your yo-yo hand so your fingers are 2 or 3 inches form the string and give the string a quick pluck with your forefinger and thumb.

○ Quickly bring your hand back, palm up and as the yo-yo rolls up the string, don't touch it, just guide it back down with a forward, downward twist of your wrists.

○ Let the yo-yo go to the bottom of the string, then pull up and catch it.

Remember to keep your eye on the yo-yo at all times!

The Bunny Hop Trouble Tips

Problem   Yo-yo comes up when you put it behind your elbow.
Cause   String is too tight.
What to Do   Loosen the string (see page 19).

Problem   You can't find the string to pluck it.
Cause   You're standing too straight and looking directly ahead.
What to Do   When you're ready to pluck, twist your head down and almost under your armpit, so you can see the string.

Problem   You pluck the string but the yo-yo won't come up.
Cause   String is too loose.
What to Do   Tighten the string by twisting the yo-yo (see page 19).
OR Cause   You're not plucking hard enough.
What to Do   Give it a good banjo twang.

Problem   You can't catch the yo-yo when the trick is done.
Cause   You're trying to catch it at the wrong time.
What to Do   Don't try to catch the yo-yo as it comes over your arm. Let it go back down first, and catch it when it comes up.

The Waterfall

○ Stand straight with your legs together. The yo-yo must be behind you in your curled hand as in The Forward Pass.

○ Swing your arm forward and let the yo-yo go straight in front of you. When it returns, do not try to catch it, just twist your hand and guide it back down between your body and your hands towards the ground. Then pull up and catch it.

The difficulty of this trick is that it cannot touch your leg, body or hand on the way back down. Sounds impossible, but with practice you can do it. See sketch below.

The Three-Leaf Clover

○ The Three Leaf Clover is just like doing three loops in a row with the following big difference:

○ Instead of all three loops being snapped out in front of you at the same height, the first loop is thrown high above in front of you. When it returns don't catch it, but curl your wrist toward your body and then snap the yo-yo out in front of you about the same height as your neck. When the yo-yo returns don't catch it, just guide it down in front of you almost like the last loop in The Waterfall. Now when it returns, you can catch it. See sketch below.

Rock the Baby

Time to learn the most popular trick in yo-yo history!

○ Throw a fast sleeper.

○ With your free hand, grab the string about halfway down.

○ Reach your yo-yo hand below your free hand and pinch the string between your index finger and thumb.

○ Reverse your catch by putting your top hand down and your bottom hand up.

○ Open your fist without losing the string. The string should take the shape of a triangle.

○ If your yo-yo is still spinning fast and straight, swing the yo-yo in and out of the cradle.

○ On the last swing, release the string from both hands. The yo-yo should come back to you all wound up.

Rock the Baby Tips and Tricks

Problem Yo-yo comes up when you grab it.
Cause String is too tight.
What to Do Loosen the string (see page 19).
OR Cause Your grabbing motions are too rough or choppy.
What to Do Relax. Make your moves fast and smooth.

Problem String knots up when trick is over.
Cause You're making triangle design wrong.
What to Do Try making the design with a yo-yo that is "dead"—or not spinning.
OR Cause In-and-out motion is wrong.
What to Do If yo-yo starts to swing from the front, it must exit from the front. If it starts to swing from the back, it must exit from the back.

That's the last trick. There are plenty of others to learn, but if you can do all the tricks in this book, you're well on your way to mastering the art of the yo-yo!

About the Author

World famous yo-yo champion **Larry Sayco** was born in Rhode Island. As a kid, he loved sports, but was too short for basketball, too light for football, and too nervous for baseball. When he saw a yo-yo pro at a boy's club, Larry knew it was the sport for him.

After high school, Larry went to work for Duncan, the world's largest yo-yo manufacturer. He was soon touring "Around the World" for them, showing off yo-yo tricks. Later, he invented and patented his very own yo-yo, the Sayco Tournament Yo-Yo. After 55 years as a pro, Larry still loves his job.

Larry Sayco
1 Sunset Ave.
Cumberland, RI 02864
(401) 724-5296
www.larrysayco.com